The Naughts

poems by

Lindsay Bell

Finishing Line Press
Georgetown, Kentucky

The Naughts

Copyright © 2017 by Lindsay Bell
ISBN 978-1-63534-198-0 First Edition
All rights reserved under International and Pan-American Copyright Conventions.
No part of this book may be reproduced in any manner whatsoever without written permission from the publisher, except in the case of brief quotations embodied in critical articles and reviews.

ACKNOWLEDGMENTS

I would like to thank my friends, family, readers, and teachers whose support and encouragement through some harrowing times made this book possible. Special thanks to: c.h. eding, Becca Klaver, Ben Niemi & Daniela Olszewska, for giving of your time to read this introvert poet. And a big, broad-shouldered thank you to the poets of Columbia College Chicago, particularly David Trinidad, and to pogroup: your influence streams from the flatlands and has helped me find a foothold in the mountains.

Thank you to Christen Kincaid and the staff at Finishing Line Press for helping me to bring my poems further into the world.

Publisher: Leah Maines

Editor: Christen Kincaid

Cover Art: Mitch Weller

Author Photo: Mitch Weller

Cover Design: Elizabeth Maines McCleavy

Printed in the USA on acid-free paper.
Order online: www.finishinglinepress.com
          also available on amazon.com

                Author inquiries and mail orders:
                       Finishing Line Press
                          P. O. Box 1626
                    Georgetown, Kentucky 40324
                              U. S. A.

Table of Contents

I Belong to You 1
Ode to the Apple 2
Danse Macabre 3
Streber 4
Cold Snap 5
Love Did This 6
Bicycle 7
Dead Tongues 8
Ghost Anniversary 9
Incorporation Certificate 10
Forgot How to Suffer 11
Lovesong of the Mountaineer 12
This One Old Trick to Live Forever 13
Lux Aeterna 14
Oops 15
Bearing Gifts 16
Death as an Academic Exercise 17
Sleepers, Wake 18
Pauline 19
Proximity 20
Baby Doe 21
Margin Architecture 22
Appropriate Placement 23
A Sculpture of Human Ashes 24
In Which All Your Dreams Are Shot in the Head and
    Survive 25

for Mitch—my favorite geologist

I Belong to You

Not for want of effort
we do not speak of it.
Unresponsive granite.

I snore in the tent,
take breaths steady
yet incoherent, a touch
raspy with age or climate.

I have licked so many rocks
with my rough tongue,
slept through storms'
booming echoes.

A hiker is struck by lightning
on his honeymoon.
What the air does
to permanence, to appease.

Ode to the Apple

For the wanderer who forgot
    how to turn a phrase
    who wants our love;
For the wretch whose apathy
    ate her coreless,
    puckered;
For we can aspirate
    the earth
    but we need a conduit
    to get the worms
    out of our will;
For the snake,
    in careful netting
    on the banks of the Clear Creek
    rattling;
For the dogs cocking their heads,
    backed away,
    while their humans
    inclined to their doom;
For in the ever closer, wherein
    something lies coiling—
    indomitable;
For the utter giving in of predator
    and prey, entwined
    and equal,
    without blame or conceit.

Danse Macabre

In the celebrity graveyard
of my dreams, loneliness

marked on a stone
whereon is perched

Nevermore—

I squawk at the bird,
which does not reply.

Aren't I important enough
to be guarded by nothing?

The great equalizer, they call him,
outmoded as a scythe,
and not to be outdone.

Streber

Today I smelled the summer's
sad last batch of freedom fries

heard the ice cream truck hemiola
whose pitch unwinds with each iteration.

As I pull into the driveway
rain begins to plunk in the gutters

in seamless concord with ending.

All the unhappiest children
scream the loudest,

having the most neon
artifice.

All 40 of the world's saddest
mothers weep recitations

into their handkerchiefs
of different points in the same conversation.

Cold Snap

No rest for the willing machine

but your hubs froze
chain case cracked in the air so cold
it chapped your ass through your jeans
sapped all the fluids from your fingertips
swollen with the laziest blood.

You said you felt like you were having a heart attack
next to the Walgreen's
as you forced your highest stuck gear
up to the Ulysses roundabout, sucking 15° so hard.

All this pavement scraping for my sake, I think,
and once the wheel puts into motion, easy enough
to stay.

Love Did This

I'd been kidding myself with play fear
but real fear just woke me up,
put a robe on my nakedness, yoked me again.

It said, Lo, I am the toaster
in the bathtub
of your performance anxiety,
the real projector,
the spit and glare and cross yourself.

I am your mother's weary voice,
the faint hearing test intoning right
then left, I am the singsong of baby's breath
carpeting a grave,

I am the burden of you
who are my slave.

Bicycle

Let's ride out to meet
the dread of the world

teetering on Dinosaur Ridge—
you can't say we've parted

with anything special
as it's never been.

I put it out of my mind every night
in anticipation of stripping it

out of my body
by needless work in the morning.

I can never attack the climb
as you do,

but no matter—
I know I have the handicap

having to empty out each night
as I do.

Dead Tongues

You had no gift for Greek
yet sent your emissaries
of grief into me.

Imagine rape as a theft
of letters : I'm writing through holes
in the alphabet.

We dance about and thwart one another
favorite position : pen pal

It's a trope : a chink in the wall
through which only epistles
should have purchase.

Ghost Anniversary

What I have given away could fill a tomb with letters.
But it's none of it real.
Epochs mock our alreadys and evers,
something like nevers.

The cat motorboats on the sideboard.
Meaning content or afraid.
Such a narrow spectrum.

I stare at my face in the sliding glass door,
looking almost human.
I wait for it to visit in earnest.

I am in contact with the only everlasting thing : no.
And I should be sad and remorseful
and ashamed.
But I delight at this full-bodied apparition : she
has broken through, gray and guilty
and full of good stories, at last.

Incorporation Certificate

I'm neither salt nor salted, though often I look back
(become a pillar)
only to see files I've yet to file :
the many taxonomies of refusal.

Legally our bodies were made one body, like fantastic beasts
of medieval travelogues. The headless one,
the torso for a head, the dead-eyed savage
amalgam of truncated limbs. The lion man. The man lion.

All conflation : *Quid pro quo qui locutus est.*
How in the desert sand gets everywhere,
such that every grain is a signatory.
The signature—its crux of joining
disjoints me, seems designed
to disappoint. It's the sweet of ink
pretending totality between us.

Forgot How to Suffer

Some sick red tinsel twinkles in faux Spring.
As though a dying breath, it fries in the breeze.
It's 70° and in the East,
prophecies of burial by snow come to pass.

Meanwhile, my dry grass provides a magnetic West,
stiff and American as corn pone. Foothills
shrug off that December weakness.
Eventually, all come from afar to arrive.

Is this then our arrival, I wonder.
A frontier ballad, estranged from itself,
rising from abroad. I imagine its translation
suggests we've been saying *literally* too much.

Lovesong of the Mountaineer

I am mounted
on the cusp of the former,
surveying damage done the latter.
I map these intangible outcroppings,
abstract changes : what is glacial skirting,
what is alluvial, what is lava flow.

I trace and interrogate the angles
between us.
Not to disrupt their ancient
materials, nor to revise them—
they are as new as their predecessors old.

What is old as the earth, I think.
Is its demands : the body intrepid,
the mind limber.
The more points we mark,
the more precisely we map.

It is summitless, hovering
between touch
and rejoinder, pen and page,
time-sealed scar and enigma of force :
the fierce element
that has brought us to face
rock sheer and boulder field.

This One Old Trick to Live Forever

Look, I quit cereal years ago,
but I still watch the commercials.

Such triviality requires no celestial will,
no, nor jacket, just the quiet burrowing hunger
for over-sweetened grains.

For I feel the ferocious deadlines of other people's lives
hovering on dusty desks and bedside tables
quickening to wake cultivated names.

For as all the notebook paper
wasted on cootie catchers
adorns the 8th grades of my twilight dreams.

For as dreams compose
themselves to incarnate fragments
in the ramparts of memory.

For as memory begets loss.

For as bodies so easily forget
their own names,
they must tear out the new ones.

Lux Aeterna

Raw mercy of the unjoined world,
the hour when night looks a little peaky,
and the earth, so swollen with its dead that it must
live, or explode.

My bougie tea steaming, I listen to the kind of jazz
they play before the birds have lit off for a day
of climbing wind and hitching various currents.

I hope to stay in this time of dumbness, brimming
with possibility, expecting nothing.

Oops

Sometimes things break and we couldn't be happier.
In a hurry to get to the next place we don't know yet
and the phone rings, a baby cries, somebody's pregnant.
Pop music loves this shit but jazz couldn't be bothered
any more than Bix could coax Louis home
before he was done talking to the press.

Two rings and straight to voicemail.
On and on, our fixation on fluids keeps us base,
the way water expands to fit its container,
we're kept making tick marks in whatever column
till it gets fixed. But there are no fuckups in jazz.

Bearing Gifts

Vague muttering in the next room
outbursts of grown-ups playing at hearts,
subdued by a glimmer of reminiscences,
fluttering bible pages, dogeared at Ruth.
Whither thou goest, I shall go.

It happened as it was meant to, at an appropriate time.
Christmas, between harvests, her favorite number,
before a storm, by the barn, or in the attic,
after a shower, feeding the kittens, sweeping the porch.
All the bills in a stack, scrawled on in spidery script
their due dates, when they were paid.

Now gone, the pansy-rimmed plates
on their spindled plate rails, gone
the dollar bills from their cool whip pails
paid for bringing in the eggs.
Gone, all gone to the auction house
the green glass candy dishes, the dusty cushions,
the creased white pocket squares, gone.

The older she grew, the less tragic her leavings,
more museum pieces than the daily prayers
and intentions of hands so translucent,
so much nearer a ghost than anything real,
as to be a miracle.

Who's to say she wasn't too young to die?
Who's to say too old to live?
A box of ash decides the living debt to dead.
I pretend to teach the earth
something it already knows : how to reproduce.
I attempt to say *look here* and *ring this bell*
and *genuflect* because I know I'm nothing
I'm part of it all, I'm everything.
Because I'm here, I'm gone, gone, gone.

Death as an Academic Exercise

Rigmarole of rigor
mark'd whereon I stood
upon a stone and with flagging
cadence (circadian rhythm
damned lectures after lunchtime
office hrs.) conducted
the thought experiment
by my nose, diving into Donne.

Sleepers, Wake

They came to me fitful
all crying out at once
and would not be placated
by Bach.
        We want to be rocked, they said.
I am half-joking, half-serious.
I am all serious, super-serious.
        I address the wantons
like my sister unbegotten.
        I address their workshop
like a waking nightmare
crying, can't you make shoes
or gloves, can't you cover
yourselves with industry?
        I address them as though
they had never seen the way stars
cannot sit still
though they've been dead
for millennia.
        I address them though they
do not know what it is to make love
to a stranger.
        I address them, my voice
a servants' gong, a dirge, a war-horn blast,
the union of flesh and pulp,
the divorce unsubdued
of unknowing from bliss.

Pauline

You come hither or get out
into the electromagnetic mutter,
stuck between
even your echoes, shivering
rhetorical turn, but.

Once you've put names to the tricks,
there's no use remaining a ghost.

We share a common lineage,
approaching dust like a prudent housewife.
Vacuum incessantly, buff windowglass
with warm breath (avoid fingering hearts),
skirt hedges, always a half leaf off perfection.

In the attic, there's a hope chest of no use,
a book of deep maroon that's not been lifted in five years
but which we must keep, embarrassed
the way we each keep to our bodies.

Proximity

I was born with a historical gap.

All my clothes were fitted for it,
pink and asymmetrical.

I was a pink lobster, lop-sided meringue,
chewed air with my hands, ruined my toes.

The floor wept under me.
I was timing.

Allergic to gift horses,
all glossy, candied things.

I was crocheted into a name, sing-song.
The picture of innocence : a tutu in danger.

Baby Doe

Hers a belly in which
no mystery is possible
nor succor in her pyrite mouth

two trains meet in a word problem
and 52 girls get pulled
from their early marriage beds

light slits open
tedious rescue
her fate redundant

she pans the prospectors
peers into all the pools
copious and clear

she will begin again
with a slightly different
spelling and a teasing comb.

Margin Architecture

Later faults dismember our early geometries,
        a failed arm wastes, leaving the mark
        of its absence
commonly bounded by angular unconformities.
        Blue abides in everything, slashed with black,
        dots of light pock our walls.
We are the consequence of erosion, or a poor seismic pick.
        Our earliest memories of water,
        captive to heave and throw, strike and slip.
A sequence of calcareous mudstones and marls
        sum our lifetime moments,
        some marine transgression, resultant desertification.
Submarine channeling
        bespeaks burrowing creatures, deposited
        by meandering, fixed by their outlines.
A topographic map : cipher of our hinterlands
        interbedded basement interactions
        created a seam, fingers lace with blue.
Volcanoclastic sadness, the minor plays of Shakespeare.
        Dust motes deposit in geologic time as we hover,
        watch the names they've given us
Attempt to interpret themselves.

Appropriate Placement

There is a dentist next to the liquor store;
The alcoholic receives a reminder.

The hype machine exists to encourage (fees).
Vancouver is so classy. So, so classy.

Bananas should be the most visible,
all our movements timed to like decay.

Kiss me in the burning streets, comfort
me in my needless angst.

We're only happy when we're encased,
locked and latched. We are free.

I have ignored the fine weather to follow
the storylines of ludicrous disaster films.

In the course of a working day,
I watch L.A. become a volcano three times.

A ghost follows me, folds my clothes,
hangs out and makes me tea.

All one can hope for in the afterlife
is a benevolent master.

A Sculpture of Human Ashes

If I could harness the rapidity of change
at ten thousand feet
I would have made a museum of myself.
A shade of purple so much so it is no longer purple.

I am devoted to that moment of hello,
so much because it is the embryo of goodbye.
It does not look like a tiny person built
of tissue and genetic material,
for a tiny person wants only to know
what it means to fail, the verisimilitude of nature
to a tiny person, how all things break.

Each season will erase me from it :
slashes of scorched Aspen stands in March,
snow in June, alpenglow.

In Which All Your Dreams Are Shot in the Head and Survive

You tease them out
squirming like viscera shocked
by a sudden vivisection

This is for your own good
This is for your own good

As you would say to a child
while trying to convince
yourself of surety

How does a bullet always
manage to fly into every absence?

Lindsay Bell is a poet based near Denver, Colorado. She obtained a BA in English from Luther College (Decorah, IA) and an MFA in Creative Writing-Poetry from Columbia College Chicago. She is the author of the chapbook *Signs Point to Yes* (dancing girl press). Her work has appeared in Barrelhouse, DIAGRAM, H_NGM_N, Puerto del Sol, Spinning Jenny and elsewhere. She is also a classically-trained soprano and can often be found singing with various choirs throughout the Denver metro area.

www.ingramcontent.com/pod-product-compliance
Lightning Source LLC
LaVergne TN
LVHW041517070426
835507LV00012B/1646